White Blood

White

A Lyric of Virginia

Blood

KIKI PETROSINO

SARABANDE BOOKS Louisville, KY

Library of Congress Cataloging-in-Publication Data

Names: Petrosino, Kiki, 1979– author.
Title: White blood : a lyric of Virginia / Kiki Petrosino.
Description: First edition. | Louisville, KY : Sarabande Books, 2020.
Identifiers: LCCN 2019032278 (print) | LCCN 2019032279 (e-book)
ISBN 9781946448545 (paperback) | ISBN 9781946448552 (e-book)
Subjects: LCSH: African American women—Poetry.
Women—Identity—Poetry. | Virginia—Poetry.
Classification: LCC PS3616.E868 A6 2020 (print) | LCC PS3616.E868 (e-book)
DDC 811/.6—dc23
LC record available at https://lccn.loc.gov/2019032278
LC e-book record available at https://lccn.loc.gov/2019032279

Cover and interior design by Alban Fischer.
Manufactured in Canada.
This book is printed on acid-free paper.
Sarabande Books is a nonprofit literary organization.

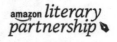

This project is supported in part by an award from the National Endowment for the
Arts. The Kentucky Arts Council, the state arts agency, supports Sarabande Books
with state tax dollars and federal funding from the National Endowment for the Arts.

Contents

pay attention to
what sits inside yourself
and watches you

—LUCILLE CLIFTON

Prelude

You're on a train & your ancestors are in the Quiet Car.

The Quiet Car is locked with a password you can't decrypt.

You're a professional password decrypter, but your ancestors are demolition experts.

You're wearing black tactical gear & your ancestors are wearing black tactical gear.

You're dashing through each compartment, slamming doors open, while your ancestors lay small explosives.

As heat expands within the carriage, you escape through a picture window.

You climb to the top of the train & your ancestors rappel down the sides.

You're rappelling down one side of the train when you glimpse your ancestors above you.

They leap from carriage to carriage as if weightless, as if drifting, as if curling tongues of snow.

You cling to the side of the train as each of your ancestors lifts away from you.

They float into the cloud of themselves.

In the rushing light, you perceive them as hundreds of slow snake doctors.

0—

you begin.

What Your Results Mean:

Western Africa 28%

1.

The West African   you

                        is   a

        hunter

        try

try

carry this

2.

The West African   you   has

split

                                    and

    expanded

                            A mixture
                                historic

                    as

            a   gene

3.

The West African component of your

                                  lineage. The

           "Out of Africa" event

                  the

                            New World slave

               seen in

             this genetic   print

4.

you

are likely

A mixture

a   cluster

a

high number

5.

                      your DNA has roots that

          cluster and

     spread

              and

trade

       and

     carry

6.

The West African   you
                    spanning

                        more than

                              more

7.

regions of

time

in people

o-

8.

between this cluster and

              this cluster

   an

African   o

       o, **Niger and Chad**

      o   fingerprint

9.

African   you
                    span   most of
                    Africa. African America
African Diaspora
                    and the
            Southern African forests
            "Out of Africa"

            east, south, and then southeast. Within

Africa   throughout Africa
                                the historic

African

world

10.

well

so   so

well

so

Happiness

I.

In. I got in. That is, inland
to the inmost place, my University
blue ink on the letterhead
orange slit in my thumb
in the innards of each finger pad
so deep, you could not prize me
out of my acceptance, how
I prized the letter they let me
in with, into that indwelling spot
where I grew like a braid
in bad light, in some bind—
honors of Honor, my crown
grew all season. Circlet of torches
blooming on the hill.

2.

Blooming across hills, I was
a girl of blooming sense. Of slip
& colored sedge. A floret.
The stem of my neck spiked
up from my lanyard. My head
leaned & looped sunward.
Back then, my body filled a chair
—plant body, water body—
back then, in that weedy way
—seed girl, scholarship girl—
but I didn't feel it, didn't yet
sense myself turning into sedge grass
spiraling from the root
blade upon blade upon blade.

3.

Blade upon blade upon blade
a Cavalier grows. In here
the colonnade *clink* of goblets.
A Cavalier loves her universe:
slashes, shadowed stripes.
She looks center right, or center
justified. She seeks that middle
note some never reach. White heart
of the page, where distinguished men
appear in battalions of charm.
They will not speak to thee. *How
to write, with only thick white ink
& not be thought a cheat?* We think
& think. We think & think & think.

4.

To think! Of those white kids
whose turn (some said) I took.
I took it hard.
My turn, my breath.
My package of aid. I made
a massive shape
mid-traipse across the Lawn
or hunched at lunch. I ate
the beautiful books I bought
with borrowed funds
& swallowed down
that two-ness *one ever feels*.
My body's debt: silent slab.
I knew I was a living lab.

5.
Since I was a living lab
I scythed, skull-clean
my crop of hair.
I buttoned up
my button-downs like tarps
& hummed in botanical Latin
the notes of my glasshouse
erudition. Now I can't stop
counting these dents in my ribs
system of stinging whorls
tiny rosettes stelled in my side
for I leaned
so long against that trellis
what I took for petals were scars.

6.

What I took for petals
were scars. What I thought
was Jefferson was Jefferson
Park Avenue. At ten
o'clock on a Tuesday, what
I thought was just Tuesday
was my grandfather in Brooklyn
looping the cord about his neck
testing its clear, tensile
mettle before he hanged
himself. What happens when
the beloved body hangs up
its flowers? Every flower falls
over the top of the door.

7.

At the choir leader's door
I hung, offering guests
chilled shrimp bites
woodsy darts of rosemary.
I waited with the tray
she'd given me & peered
back through her faculty Pavilion.
Arrangement of deepening grids:
silver, silver, silk. One whole
chamber just for books. With
my eyes, I robbed it bare. No one
saw me chomp the chandelier.
It went down, a carnival onion.
My jaws grew: salt-sharp & strange.

8.

Let my jaws be His salt shovels.

Let my eyes be His cannonball clock.

Let my feet be the dark birds He keeps in a cloud.

Make my chest His chinaberries, their medicinal ring.

Make of my side His smokehouse smell

& my arms His lettuce, dipped in French light.

Turn my scalp blue from the smoke of His fires.

My debts, at lunch—let them be His glass doors.

Turn my neck into His turning buffet.

Ain't my breath His dumbwaiter loaded with wine?

Ain't my thoughts His nail rod, His ice house, His pond?

Look at my skin, nearly shell-edged—O

still this rattle, my heart. Bone dominoes at night.

This rasp in my heart, red leather, His swiveling throne.

9.

Ha ha, my heart, red feather of joy.
Ha! Academical Village! *Ha ha*, diversity.
Ha! Direct Loans. *Ha ha*, poetry!
Ha ha ha Eurydice's pierced foot & *ha!* My ears
pierced with white stars. *Ha*, thesis! *Ha ha ha*
Distinguished Major! My parents divorcing, *ha!*
Ha! My mother's secret apartment, plastic smell
of burnt-out headphones, *ha ha ha*, diploma, *ha ha!*
Ha ha, library, where I cried for a year & *ha*
Financial Aid, where I cried for two. *Ha ha!* My aid
disbursing a few late coins. *Ha*, cutting my hair & crying.
Ha ha! My grandfather laid out in his black suit
his collar pinched too high on his neck, remember
in Camelot, how the great thorn trees wept?
         Words & blood, words & blood, *ha ha!*

10.

In Camelot, the great thorn trees wept
over the green page of land. Remember
how light dawned in chapters.
There, the hems of our garments soaked
in promissory rain. Deep within those
snake-bright grottoes, many vines bore
their fruits of salt & wood. Water &
salt & the smell of books—in Camelot
we cannot live without books.
All of us runaways know
each other by our paper cuts. Our blood
inks the dark map of the mountains.
Ask me if I believe in forgiveness.
I do, I say. *But it is rare.*

II.

I believe in the rare—
how some trees decay with pressure
then resurrect as jet.
I believe in mineral lozenges
formed in the hot black throats
of pine forests, & in the hard belt
pine forests make
as they buckle, at long last
over the beloved larynx.
In the Theory of the Beloved
the living make do with tiny lights.
We wake up in the deep hours
to track where the body has gone:
gem of empty air, brilliant among violets.

12.

Gem of empty air, my grandfather
brilliant among violets now. Here
his green shadow condenses.
When I return to his room
trying to cross—that door—
I'm permitted only clouds
of dark leaves, only blossoms
& bee-song: *so, so, so.* He made
that door—*so, what?*—his gallows
gibetto or *orto.* Made a glass lasso.
O astonishment of glass—*O* pain—
O knowledge, shivering by
my little votive in this stanza where
Grandpa will not stay, or let me, either—

13.

My grand pain won't stay, or let me
pull it into order. So I keep ordering
my memories hard-scrambled.
Mine is that pool of slow gold
scraped down to cheerfulness. Mine
that serpentine wall, the forgetting
about crying. Gold look of the air
gathered between mountains, mine too
that graduation in mud before
the Rotunda's bare belfry.
Who knew me then, yolk-in-shell?
In whose wagons did I ride safe
in my straw nest? Neat trick, close shave.
How was *I* the dream, the hope, of the slave?

14.

How was *I* their dream, their hope?
Born too late to know them or walk
the perimeter of their graves
deep in the next county, next
planet, where I couldn't read the land
or speak the right words in the woods.
I almost drowned in the woods.
Trees turned to water. My head slurred
so I couldn't tell up from down.
How could they ever dream of me
that first ravenous morning on Grounds
my face a bright vine, twisting south
back along the way they had come
to seek the dreadful light?

15.

Blooming on the hill
blade upon blade upon blade
I think of flowers
in their living labs. I know
about scars. They become petals
falling over the door.
A door, a jaw: salt-sharp & strange.
But remember the heart, its red swivel?
Remember the great thorn trees of Camelot?
I do, I say. *But they were rare.*
Gems of violence, brilliant in space.
Camelot will not stay, or let me, either.
How am I the one they dreamed?
I go dreadful, seeking an inland light.

Albemarle

Instructions for Time Travel

You must go through Mr. Jefferson
along his row of chinaberry trees

behind the ruined smokehouse
in unmarked tracts, under fieldstones

with no carvings, no monuments
with a few leaves shadowing the mulch

near scattered weeds, in sunken lines
while the sun walks in the day

at the end of the day
in an oval of brushed earth

just as the soft path finishes
under branches

where the dead are always saying
what they always say:

Write about me.

Monticello House Tour

What they never say is: Mr. Jefferson's still
building. He's just using clear bricks now
for his turrets & halls, for the balconies
rounding his palace in transparent loops
of dug air. After death, it's so easy
to work. No one sees him go out
from the Residence, his gloves full
of quiet mortar. Mr. Jefferson's coat is narrow
as daybreak. His long sleeves drag in the muck
as he minces his turf. You know the room
you were born in? It's part of the tour. Hundreds
of rooms unfolding for miles, orchards alive
in the parlor. Remember that gold chair you loved
the one with a face like a lion, especially
in late winter, when Mother sat with you
in her pink gown, humming? As it happens
Mr. Jefferson built you that lion. He drew
your time in prudent proportions. You have one
job: to fit the design he keeps spinning.
Your whole life is laced through a ring
of similar finds. Look, it's all mothers
in pink gowns, humming.

If You Tell Them Sally Hemings
Was Three-Fourths White

They'll ask how dark she looked. When you compare her memory
      to an earthen porringer, brimming with late sun, they'll say

Fetch that porringer. Now. They'll make you fill it up with rain
      so they can regard themselves. You'll watch them swerve

their visages. As they regard themselves, they might
      mark a thing or two. They'll probably mark a thing or two

which makes them shiver. *But how'd you say she looked*
      they'll ask, patting their foreheads. *Not like you since*

you're twice as black. Of course, that's not quite right, but as you
      open your mouth to speak, you'll catch them watching

too close. You'll want to fix a drink, then. You'll drink.
      They'll probably get sleepy. *Tell us what you know*

about Sally they'll yawn, not sensing how that story swells
      under your tongue, a sweet. Remember *sweet*, how it dissolves

their boot prints from the drive? Now try your own green lungs.
      Like this. Like this. There's many a slip.

La Cuisinière Bourgeoise

Menon, 1746, Paris

Mr. Jefferson loved early green peas almost
as much I love complaining. I pick at his recipes
& their French alphabets, larded in light. We know
Mr. Jefferson loved early. Green peas, almost
translucent & gone by July. Didn't the French believe delight
& temperance marry in the mouth? I'll hold my peace
as much as I love complaining. I pick at the recipes
Mr. Jefferson loved. Early green peas, almost.

Essay in Architecture

The human face, its pine doors painted
like mahogany. Human face with horses
under each veranda. Perfect parquet tetragons
of the human face. Human face still legible
in Old French. Sealed closet of the human face
lit by oculus. Design face, tinker face, factory
face. Twine & bare wood comprising a pulley system
for the human face. Woodworked face with sunbeams
settling in. Revolving buffet supporting the human
face. Entire pewter plate collection in the face. Human
face as soup tureen, as paint chip, as spit jack. Smoke rings
textured like the human face. Human face, cured. Human
face, pickled. Human face brushed with olive oil, anchovies
& Parmesan. Green floor of the Dome Room just above
the human face. Floating view of the face, its quarter farms.
Rough cabins dotting a sloped face, partly visible. Human
face built to resemble a Great Clock. Great pendulum
drawing faces in the air.

Terrorem

Every night, I go back to Mr. Jefferson's place, searching still
his kitchens, behind staircases, in a patch of shade somewhere

beside his joinery & within his small ice house, till I get down
that pit, lined with straw, where Mr. Jefferson once stacked frozen slabs

of river water until summer. Then, visitors would come to him
to ask about a peculiar green star, or help him open up

his maps. They'd kneel together on the floor, among his books
lavish hunks of ice melting like the preserved tears

of some antique mammal who must have wept
to leave Albemarle, just as I wept when I landed in Milan

for the first time, stone city where Mr. Jefferson began
to learn the science of ice houses, how you dig into the dark

flank of the land, how you seal the cavity. Leave open
just one small hatch through which I might lift, through gratings

Mr. Jefferson's cold dressed victuals, his expensive butter & salads
the sealed jars sweating clear gems of condensation, white blood

appearing from warm air, as if air could break & slough, revealing
the curved arc of our shared Milan. There, I wore silver rings

on each thumb. I studied & spoke in fine houses
of ice. I knew a kind of crying which sealed me to such realms

for good. Old magic weep, old throb-in-throat. How much
of my fondness for any place is water, stilled & bound

to darkness?

The Virginia House-Wife

Mary Randolph, 1824, Washington, D. C.

Methodical nicety is the essence of true elegance.
To grill a calf's head, you must clean & divide it.
When the mistress gives out everything, there is
methodical nicety. The essence of true elegance
in a sauceboat, a spoonful, in a sieve. Boil it tender.
Take the eyes out whole & cut flesh from skull.
Cover these with breadcrumbs & chopped parsley.
True, essential nicety is the elegant method.
Divide a clean calf, then grill its head.

The Shop at Monticello

I'm a black body in this Commonwealth, which turned black bodies
into money. Now, I have money to spend on little trinkets to remind me

of this fact. I'm a money machine & my body constitutes the common
wealth. I spend & spend in order to support this. I support this mountain

with my black money. Strange mountain in late bloom. Strange mansion
built on mountains of wealth. I spend so much, I'm late for the tour

where I'm a blooming black dollar sign. I look good in the Dome Room
prowling its high-gloss floor. It's common to desire such flooring

for my own home, but owning a home is still strange. My blackness
makes strange tools for a living, rakes the strangeness like dirt. I like to

rake my hands over merchandise: bayberry votives, English hyssop
in crisp sachets. I like this Engraved Pewter Bookmark so much suddenly

I line up for it, clenching my upright fist. I pay cash to prove myself
no shoplifter. Still, I abscond with my black feelings: crisp toast points

dunked in fig jam. On one hand, I must think very highly of myself
to come here. Then again, that sounds like something I would say.

Souvenir

The glass lady doesn't know anything
about Sally Hemings except she was young
& got to live in Paris for two years. It doesn't
sound half bad, not when you think about it
straight-on, which nobody does, & *didn't*
they dig up a jar of French cold cream near one of the cabins
out there? The glass lady lifts candelabrum
after candelabrum in the shop whose windows
admit nothing but pewter sky. *She could've stayed*
in France & been free, but instead she got right back
on that ship with him. The glass lady's voice hums
with a harpsichord quality, just as she arrives
at *free will, she had it just like everyone.* Only now
I'm aware of the glass garden party hovering all
around us—pearl onions, champagne, & that sharp
makeup smell of grown ladies. *Isn't it really to his credit*
that she came back to live here? I feel my champagne
hatching its tiny mirrors. Perhaps it's the lady
who moves me. Amid the glass faces, I lift
my empty flute as if it's mine, as if I started it
as if I pulled, with hot tongs, a whole
orchid from the air.

Farm Book

Whenever I write about Mr. Jefferson, he gallops
over. *Knock knock,* he begins in quadruplicate. It's
pretty wild, like my student's poem about a house
of skin & hair, a house that bleeds. Mr. Jefferson's
place is so dear to me, white husk my heart beats
through, until I can't write more. In my student's
poem, the house stands for womanhood, pain coiled
in the drywall. Sorrow warps the planks, pulling nails
from ribs. In Kentucky, I'm the only black teacher
some of my students have ever met, & that pulls me
somewhere. I think of Mr. Jefferson sending his field
slaves *to the ground,* a phrase for how he made them pull
tobacco & hominy from the earth, but also for how
he made of the earth an oubliette. At sixteen, they went
to the ground if Mr. Jefferson thought they couldn't learn
to make nails or spin. He forgot about them until they
grew into cash, or more land. For him, it must've seemed
like spinning. Sorrow of souls, forced *to the ground*
as a way of marking off a plot. At sixteen, I couldn't
describe the route to my own home, couldn't pilot
a vehicle, could hardly tell the hour on an analog
clock. I had to wear my house-key on a red loop
around my neck. Now, I rush to class beneath a bronze
Confederate, his dark obelisk, his silent mustache. My books
tumble past the lectern as I recite Mr. Jefferson's litany: Swan.

Loon. Nuthatch. Kingfisher. Electric web of names, yet
in the ground, I know, a deeper weave of gone-away ones
who should mean more to me than any book. I live in language
on land they left. I have no language to describe this.

The Art of Cookery Made Plain and Easy

Hannah Glasse, 1747, Dublin

If I have not wrote in the high polite style
I hope I shall be forgiven.
If I've gripped my rawhide in the wrong hand
or if I've knotted the rope in some high polite style.
Such an odd jumble of things might spoil you for good.
The right sauce, served wrong, only glazes the error.
We all hope we shall be forgiven in high style.
Forgive the poor light where I sit, writing.

What Your Results Mean:
Northwestern Europe 12%

1.

This region

                                sh,   sh,

    sh,   sh,

                    early
              episodic habit

region   divided into

         small percentages

                            of
           centuries.

2.

                                                    it is a
                                                long

    advent

        we now know

3.

      region of   rope

                                  much more

than a
        region

              the spread of

          This

      in small   ages

4.

avian   man

migrating   south and east

Over the last

Latin

centuries.

5.

This region of
composite

        character

          grew from   mix

                and   tic

6.

O

ion   subdivided into

Empire

7.

                                                            much more
than an   historical population, it is

                                    the south

                                                ethnic   political

    so   small

8.

This region   a   graphical

                              character

                                                            o,

settler   farmer   O

                              bio   graphical region

                   of   1

9.

This region

of glaciation

spread of

settlers   the last

people of European ancestry

from
that we   part

10.

region

migrating from

region

Louisa

In Louisa

You wake up because
    you hear someone singing

little lamb, little lamb
    as if the singer were calling

from across a great
    distance. You know, as you've always

known, that you're the *little lamb*
    in this song, just as you know

that no matter how far
    you may wander from the loop

of sand where you were born
    the singer of this particular song

will always sing *little lamb* meaning you
    quite distinctly. As you

slowly climb from the covers
    you try to tell the song to *stop*

that noise, please but what comes out is
　　　play it again, which you hadn't meant

to say, at all. Soon, the song starts up
　　　once more, spinning the long journey

of itself. It speaks of coiling into thickets
　　　of sharp weeds, of slanting across hills.

The song even describes you
　　　in some time before remembrance.

You wore a suit of woven water
　　　& learned to speak in rippling syllables.

You, or someone like you.

A Guide to the Louisa County Free Negro & Slave Records, 1770–1865

The first box is for all the good white men. The ones who freed their slaves on Christmas. It's always Christmas in the first box. The day Delpha shall go out. The day Viney shall go out. These good white men *only desire the guardian care of those under age.* After that, they shall go out, just as Winney shall go out at the age of twenty-one *entirely free from me or mine or any other person whatsoever.* Delpha, Viney, & Winney shall go out on Christmas Day. The first box slides open to show their certificates. The good white men of this county *believing that all men are by nature equally free* have left many of these. One certificate is for Viney. One for Winney. One for Delpha. But these good white men can only free the slaves they truly own. One man observes *the above mentioned negroes are disputed in their titles to me, namely Delpha, Viney, & Winney.* He doesn't say more about the dispute. He doesn't say what happens on Christmas Day. This good white man has said all three should go out precisely on Christmas Day, but now it is different. It's very different now, even though Christmas has come. The good white man writes *I only free as to my right & title given under my hand.* The box slides open to show certificate after certificate. It's Christmas.

Message from the Free Smiths of Louisa County

You want to know who owned us & where.
But when you type, your searches return no results.
Bondage was grown folks' business, then old folks'.

We saw no reason to hum Old Master's name
to our grandchildren, or point out his overgrown gates
but you want to know who owned us & where

we got free. You keep typing our names into oblongs
of digital white. You plant a unicode tree & climb up
into grown folks' business. You know old folks

don't want you rummaging here, so you pile sweet jam
in your prettiest dish. You light candles & pray:
Tell me who owned you & where

I might find your graves. Little child, we're at rest
in the acres we purchased. Those days of
bondage were old folks' business. The grown folks

buried us deep. Only a few of our names survive.
We left you this: sudden glints in the grass.
The rest is grown folks' business we say. Yet
you keep asking who owned us.

Louisa County Patrol Claims, 1770–1863

I pry open the files, still packed
    with liquor & strange brine.

Midnight seeps from the cracks
    slow pulp of arithmetic. Four or five

or six at a time, the white men draw
    along the Gordonsville Road, on foot

or on horseback, clustered close—
    each man counting up his hours, the knife

of each man's tongue at the hinge
    of his own mouth. For ninety-three years

& every time I slip away to read
    those white men line the roadway

secreting themselves in the night air
    feeding & breathing in their private

column. Why belly up to their pay stubs
    scraping my teeth on the chipped flat

of each page? This dim drink only blights me
    but I do it.

The Origins of Butler Smith

B is for *bright*. A boy. No
    birthmarks but his hair

(*inclined to straightness*) &
    his nose (*more like a white man's*).

B, also, for the bluets you dreamed
    crowding the drive leading up

to the old farm you've crossed
    two states to see. What'll you do if

you find no parcel in the name of *B*?
    At the courthouse, in the relic room

at the indicated plat? So sorry you don't
    already know the yard where chickens

pecked & patted under the eye
    of Granddaddy *B*. So sorry you missed him

on his way. He must be burning high
    above your head, a comet, or worse.

The story of a comet somebody told you.
     Wrong comet, wrong county.

Wrong dates spiraled into the roll book.
     A roll of microfilm for every year you can't

confirm. How to confirm a certain smokehouse
     not marked on any grid?

Lucky *B*, spangled *B*—
     this is not where you begin.

Message from the Free Smiths of Louisa County

You ask why we didn't register as required
why we failed to appear before the Provost Marshal
why we avoided the courthouse, the census, the bank.

You ask where we sheltered while battles seethed
where our mothers gave birth, in which hidden houses
& why we didn't register as required.

While so many perished in other counties
or raged with Nat in Southampton, how did we manage?
We avoided the courthouse, the census, the bank.

Whatever we had, we held. Whatever we knew
we told no one who counted. We kept back
our names. We didn't register as required.

When you search for us now, you find silence.
You may trace us back to a moment. No further.
We avoided the courthouse, the census, the bank

with its clock, tracking everyone's time but our own.
We chose inward passages. We kept deep counsel.
We didn't register as required, which disappoints you.
Why do you trust the courthouse, the census, the bank?

The Origins of Harriett Smith

Old Master writes her name in his ledgers
  or might. It depends on what Old Master sees

what subtleties he tracks, which gifts. *Suki walked*
  to Jerdone, he writes, but you need to read

Harriett walked. You need her to come up
  from the quarter & step through the narrow

bell of Old Master's attention, *a light girl*
  with ears bored for rings. But Harriett is prudent.

She never wastes her scant yard of brown
  ticklenburg or breaks her tools in the field.

For a whole page in his daybook, instead of writing
  about Harriett, Old Master counts

his glass decanters from France. He orders
  every hand to finish harvest without saying whose.

You search for Harriett until the yellow
  globes of Old Master's script go dim, gummed

like the fallen seedpods about his house. Well, well.
It's a good thing you're a finch now.

You were born to gorge.

Mrs. A. T. Goodwin's Letter to the Provost Marshal, 1866

You ask why I raised my hand to that boy, why
I gave him some raps over the head, you ask
why I took my small riding whip to his shoulders
his head, why, you ask, when he would not cut logs
at the woodpile. You ask why I took him by the hand &
gave him some raps, when not one stick did he cut from twelve
to four. I told his mother, my milker washer, I told her
in plain words he must do better. I told her all this without
any improvement. She was insolent, which is why my son
struck her. He only struck her when she ran from her cabin
to pluck up the boy while I was giving him some raps
over the head & shoulders with just my small riding
whip. Understand, Sir, this boy had not cut more than
two scant handfuls of wood for my cookstove, but all
the family were engaged to me: his mother, the boy
to bring my horses to water, to cut wood, only yesterday
he said *I shall not cut a stick of wood. I shall not touch it.* So these
are the negroes we've raised, never abused a single one, always
had the kindest feelings, the kindest, so long as their conduct
were tolerable, so long as I did not have to stand
by my woodpile, smelling the woodpile, the smell of the sap
intolerable from twelve to four, the heave & snap of the clear
sap inside the logs, never holding still, so that I had rather stand

in the house, my hands sifting flour across a board, so that
in truth I had much rather be still, holding nothing but
my riding whip, dark & folded up small.

The Estate of Butler Smith

They say his house had so many wings
        it looked like a sleeping hawk. They say a family

of whitefolks must've built it. Enough verandas for everyone
        to have a secret view of the place, each railing

painted to match the trees, so you felt
        you were stepping on clear air when you went

out there with your morning tea. The whitefolks kept
        pine seeds in the cellar & gardening books

on stands in the hall. But something happened.
        They got in their wagon & said: *Take care of all this*

till we get back. Which is the only way, they say
        a man like Butler could get a house with so many

grand porches on every floor. They say: *Blacks weren't meant*
        to look down on the world from a height. Except, he did.

So you start to think of the land as his book.
        He wrote what he wished.

Message from the Free Smiths of Louisa County

We weren't truly free until
we read the amendment ourselves
all the way to Lincoln's signature, dark vines

gathering over the page. *A. Lincoln* said we
should go forth, leaving bondage forever
but we weren't truly free until

we signed our own names & read them
back to ourselves. Our names, not our marks
dark vines gathered at *X*. Lincoln's signature

looked so calm, a brown river of stones
worn smooth with patience. We had no time
to catch up. We weren't truly free until

we'd scaled the high turret of *B* or unlatched
the strap where *H* buckles itself. Still, it took years
to reach Lincoln's signature, dark vines

gathering. Our jagged serifs serrated the pages
we signed. We wrote out our wills. You write
poems about Lincoln, dark little vines of *until*.
But we weren't truly free. Read the amendment.

How It Feels to Love Butler Smith

You don't love him, exactly. You love the wagon
    of his name, long letters filling up

with leaves & peeling bark. You love walking around
    Louisa, imagining Butler's voice calling *haw!*

to his horses, a sound to strike the chilly
    cobbles at night. Almost nothing from his time

survives: the courthouse, the occasional hat rack
    in a restaurant, & those cobbles, reddish & packed

like reptile scales in the streets. Of course, the cobbles
    only look special to you because of Butler, unloading

his wagon before the post office, which blurs suddenly
    into a modern gastropub serving small

batch bourbon. How quickly your Butler, too, unfolds
    into other Butlers, each one alive in his own Louisa.

If you could reach into every successive Butler Smith
    past the springs & bolsters of his mind, you'd draw

infinite replicas of yourself, standing outside
    the gastropub, your tiny glass of bourbon

an unpainted flower bud unfolding
    time after time.

Message from the Free Smiths of Louisa County

What is it like, to have a body?
Like insects, or velvet—we almost remember.
It's why we sent you the dreams.

Something green. Something moving.
We remember holding the rain in our mouths.
We think: *It's like that, to have a body.*

Furious burst of blood from the dirt—
thousands of white seeds, falling—
it's why we sent you. The dreams

keep our wishes walking. We're lonely
without music to play in our hollow.
You still have a body. Do you like it?

We almost remember the air
in this place: silk of violets, linen of sky.
It's why we sent you the dreams

of hanging your dress in a burned house
of dissolving into our thicket.
You dream because you still have a body.
Tell us what it's like.

Heritage Tourism in Central Virginia

Say you come from a region famous for fine rural
  manor houses. Say you luck into a spa coupon

good for a weekend of *Monticello Full Body Facials*
  & *Jefferson's Herbal Retreat*.

This place is a gem of an Old South *jardin*, comfortably
  appointed. Just try an egg. A plank of pure country ham.

Just stretch your boots across
  the live oak floor. Everyone's so cheerful here

above the malarial belt & below the typhoid zone
  between states which fought a war that we won't

name just now. That rushing sound's from several
  artesian springs, & you may drink from every one.

You may sit in the center of a large shady lawn
  on a summer evening, while the proprietor sets

dozens of Japanese lanterns on little tables. Your waiter
  hands you a single oyster fork, which you're at liberty

to advance through your skull at any time.
No one here shall say a word.

Approaching the Smith Family Graveyard

Flushed with notions of freedom
you follow the old wood road to its end.
Butler's acreage opens up behind fence posts

a spill of storybook umber. Even the light
between birches feels thicker now
flushed with notions of freedom.

For a moment, you wonder if the land
will dissolve before you can rush forward.
Then you're over the fence, on Butler's acreage

where deer blinds hang like aerial masks.
You gather your private handful of acorns
flushed with emotion. Freedom is old here

despite the long aisles of trail cameras
looking down from their graying trunks.
What can harm you on Butler's acreage? Open

your stride to cover more ground. *Any
descendant may access a grave* says the law
you printed before climbing the fence.
This is freedom, for now.

What Your Results Mean:
North and East Africa 5%

I.

For millennia the

Mediterranean Sea was as one

Despite the

constant movement of people across

people

2.

This component

traveled

across
logical connection
remnants

all numb

3.

north of

the world

       the earliest people

                saw

Africa

      evident in the

   I

4.

place of
                first migration

                        mitochondrial

                                flux

                the   savannah

frequency

5.

This component of you

includes   a
                              Great Rift

                              influx of
                                   lists

6.

       Mediterranean
Mediterranean   most traveled

                                 Mediterranean
                  biological

old

                  and
                      in
            pain

7.

the   Sea

                                    saw

        the south
                                    saw the

        south

                        see

8.

south

oldest

                                            home

                            wide-open
                                    high

9.

south of the

Great   Valley and west of

Lucy

here

the   pen

10.

birthplace   as well as   departure
point

   Ocean

                this is where
Historically

   we

      from

Interlude

Psalm

Dear Lord, Dear High Remembrancer
  Dear Providential Love—have mercy.

Have mercy, thou Surveyor of Wildflowers, Assessor of Royal
  & Exquisite Bee-Realms. Have mercy, Ledger

Who Tracks Us in the Night, Who Measures without Speaking
  Our Dark Trespasses. For nothing here survives—

not the gold-legged deer, browsing the bleached office park at dawn
  nor the minute finch on her branch of long division—

but *thou thou thou* absorb it, all. O Gazer, be kind in thy absorbing
  calculus. Won't be long before thy reckoning curve

arrives at the junction of our error. How, beneath thy Mineral Eye
  we walk abroad, forgetting thee, Cartographer of Sparrows.

Acknowledgments

My research for this book was supported by the National Endowment for the Arts, the Kentucky Arts Council, the English Department at the University of Louisville, the University of Louisville's Commonwealth Center for the Humanities and Society, and by Virginia Humanities at the University of Virginia. I thank these institutions for the time and tools necessary to realize this volume.

I also wish to thank experts at the Library of Virginia, Thomas Jefferson's Monticello, and the Louisa County Historical Society for their assistance in locating the archival documents that inform some of these poems.

Versions of two poems entitled "What Your Results Mean" appeared online at *The Rumpus* on April 4, 2019.

A version of the poem "Happine∫s" appeared on-line at *Tin House* on October 23, 2018.

Versions of the poems "Instructions for Time Travel" and "Monticello House Tour" appeared in the Spring 2018 issue of *Washington Square Review*. The latter poem is reprinted in *Pushcart Prize XLIV: Best of the Small Presses*, edited by Bill Henderson (Pushcart Press, 2019).

The poems "Terrorem" and "Farm Book" appeared in the *LA Review of Books Quarterly*.

Versions of the poem "Prelude" and many of the poems in the section "Louisa" appeared in the 2017 chapbook *Black Genealogy*, published by Brain Mill Press. In January 2018, the Louisville Ballet included a version of the poem "In Louisa" in their annual Choreographer's Showcase. The piece, choreographed by Louisville Ballet dancer Shelby Shenkman, was danced by Annie Honebrink and Sanjay Saverimuttu as I recited the poem on stage.

The poem "A Guide to the Louisa County Free Negro & Slave Records, 1770–1865" appeared online at *The Nation* on November 2, 2017.

Versions of three poems, now titled "Message from the Free Smiths of Louisa County," first appeared in the Fall 2017 issue of *The Hampden-Sydney Poetry Review*.

I'm grateful to Julia Kudravetz for her continuing friendship and for her hospitality during my time as a Virginia Humanities Fellow in Charlottesville in Fall 2016. Dan Rosenberg, Mary Hickman, and Rachel Abramowitz provided crucial insights during my writing process.

My husband, Philip Miller, stayed up with me many nights as I wrote, read, worried, and wept over the poems in this book. I could not ask for a kinder or more generous partner with whom to share my life.

My mother, Patricia Petrosino, accompanied me on two long road trips to Virginia so that I could pursue my research leads. For my entire life, she has supported me with kindness, fierce intelligence, music, and strength. We've had many adventures together, and there are more to come.

Notes

This book opens with a quotation from Lucille Clifton's poem, "the message from The Ones (received in the late 70s)." This poem appears in Clifton's 2004 volume, *Mercy* (BOA Editions).

The three poems entitled "What Your Results Mean" are erasures taken from my results after I completed a National Geographic Geno 2.0 DNA Ancestry Test Kit.

The reference to "two-ness," in the fourth sonnet of "Happine/s," comes from W. E. B. DuBois's 1903 treatise, *The Souls of Black Folk*. The last line of the thirteenth sonnet reformulates a line from Maya Angelou's 1978 poem, "Still I Rise."

The poems *"La Cuisinière Bourgeoise," "The Virginia House-Wife,"* and *"The Art of Cookery Made Plain and Easy"* take their titles, and reconfigure select lines, from three popular published cookbooks of Thomas Jefferson's day. The inset notes beneath each poem's title cite the author, publication city, and year for the editions I referenced.

The titles "Essay in Architecture" and "Terrorem" come from Thomas Jefferson's own writings. In an October 10, 1809, letter to Benjamin Henry Latrobe, Jefferson referred to the neoclassical design of Monticello as his "essay in Architecture." In a June 8, 1803, letter to Thomas Mann Randolph, Jefferson ordered the sale of an enslaved boy who had been accused of attacking another boy in Jefferson's nailery.

In having the boy sold away to Georgia, Jefferson wrote that he would make "an example of him in terrorem to others." Digital versions of both letters are available at Founders Online, a collection of the National Archives (https://founders.archives.gov).

The poem "Farm Book" is dedicated to the students in my Fall 2018 advanced poetry workshop at the University of Louisville. *Thomas Jefferson's Farm Book* is a manuscript compilation of Jefferson's detailed plantation records, including references to some of the hundreds of enslaved people who worked at Monticello throughout Jefferson's life there. While the compendium is available as a book in a number of editions, the original manuscript resides in the Coolidge Collection of Thomas Jefferson Manuscripts at the Massachusetts Historical Society. A digitized version is available at https://masshist. org/thomasjeffersonpapers/farm.

Harriett and Butler Smith, mother and son, are two ancestors of mine who resided in the Green Springs neighborhood of Louisa County, Virginia, in the nineteenth and twentieth centuries. The poems in the section "Louisa" referring to these "free Smiths" are inspired as much by the documentary silences in their histories as by the existing records of their lives.

The poem "A Guide to the Louisa County Free Negro & Slave Records, 1770–1865" takes its title and reformulates some of the content from Louisa County court documents now archived at the Library of Virginia in Richmond.

The poem "Mrs. A. T. Goodwin's Letter to the Provost Marshal, 1866" takes its title and reformulates individual phrases from a handwritten letter filed at the Virginia Freedmen's Bureau Field Office in Louisa, Virginia (Roll 104, Reports and Bills of Lading, Sep. 1865–Nov. 1866, Images 163–4). A digitized microfilm version of the document is available online at https://familysearch.org.

In the poem "Heritage Tourism in Central Virginia," the phrases "Monticello Full Body Facial" and "Thomas Jefferson's Herbal Retreat" are taken from spa services available in 2019

The poem "Approaching the Smith Family Graveyard" takes one of its refrains from John Randolph Barden's 1993 PhD dissertation, "'Flushed with Notions of Freedom': The Growth and Emancipation of a Virginia Slave Community, 1732–1812," from Duke University. Barden's dissertation concerns a different episode of my ancestors' journey in Virginia, but I have taken the liberty of borrowing the line for my poem about Louisa.

The poem "Psalm" first appeared in *Louisville Magazine* on November 9, 2018 and is dedicated to Maurice E. Stallard and Vickie Lee Jones, victims of the October 24, 2018, shooting at the Jeffersontown Kroger in Louisville, Kentucky.

SARABANDE BOOKS is a nonprofit literary press located in Louisville, KY. Founded in 1994 to champion poetry, short fiction, and essay, we are committed to creating lasting editions that honor exceptional writing. For more information, please visit sarabandebooks.org.